EDGE BOOKS™

The Amazingly
GROSS Human Body

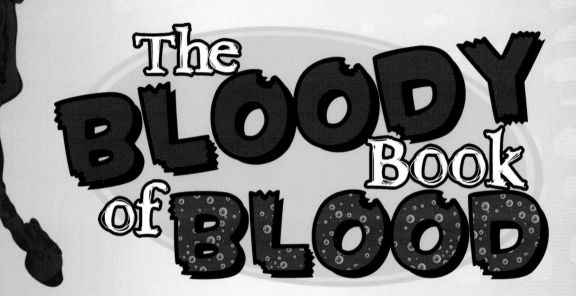

The BLOODY Book of BLOOD

by Kelly Regan Barnhill

**Consultant:**
Michael Bentley
Professor of Biology
Minnesota State University, Mankato

Capstone
press®

Mankato, Minnesota

Edge Books are published by Capstone Press,
151 Good Counsel Drive, P.O. Box 669, Mankato, Minnesota 56002.
www.capstonepress.com

*Library of Congress Cataloging-in-Publication Data*
Barnhill, Kelly Regan.
    The bloody book of blood / by Kelly Regan Barnhill.
    p. cm. — (Edge books. The amazingly gross human body)
    Summary: "Describes the gross qualities of blood, and how it works
to benefit a person's health" — Provided by publisher.
    Includes bibliographical references and index.
    ISBN 978-1-4296-3352-9 (library binding)
    1. Blood — Juvenile literature. I. Title. II. Series.
QP91.B136 2010
612.1'1 — dc22                                           2009005053

**Editorial Credits**
Aaron Sautter, editor; Kyle Grenz, designer; Jo Miller, media researcher

**Photo Credits**
Alamy/PHOTOTAKE Inc./Microworks, 11; PHOTOTAKE Inc./
    Yoay Levy, 10, 15
Capstone Press/Karon Dubke, cover (all), 4, 5, 14, 20, 21, 28, 29
Corbis RF/Reed Kaestner, 7
Getty Images Inc./Dorling Kindersley, 19 (top); Nucleus Medical Art,
    Inc., 19 (bottom)
Newscom/AFP/MSF/Pascale Zinten, 25
Photo Researchers, Inc/Dr. P. Marazzi, 22
Shutterstock/Filipe B. Varela, borders; Sebastian Kaulitzki, 16;
    Timothey Kosachev, 8; Yaroslav, 27
Superstock, Inc., 12, 13
Visuals Unlimited/Dr. Brad Mogen, 26

# TABLE of CONTENTS

# BLOOD to the RESCUE!

Imagine you're riding your bike on a beautiful day. Suddenly, your bike slides on some loose gravel. You land hard on the road and feel a sharp pain in your knees. You don't want to look. You grit your teeth and look anyway. Your skin is scraped open and red drops of blood are slowly oozing out.

We've all seen blood. It seeps out the sides of a bandage. It pours from broken noses. And it leaks out under the flap of skin on a stubbed toe. Blood is constantly running under our skin. But why is it there?

## GROSS FACT

An average adult has about 5 quarts (4.7 liters) of blood. That's more than 13 cans of soda!

# THE BODY'S HERO

Your body is made up of billions of tiny cells. Every day, your cells work hard to keep you healthy. To do their job, cells need a constant supply of nutrients, oxygen, and water. Your cells would stop working without these things, which means you would stop working too.

Something needs to carry nutrients and oxygen to your body's cells. What does this job? You guessed it — gross, disgusting blood. Blood is the icky, sticky superhero of the human body. Blood supplies your body's cells with the nutrients they need. It carries cells that fight germs and helps heal wounds. Blood even helps regulate your body's temperature.

# WHAT is this RED STUFF?

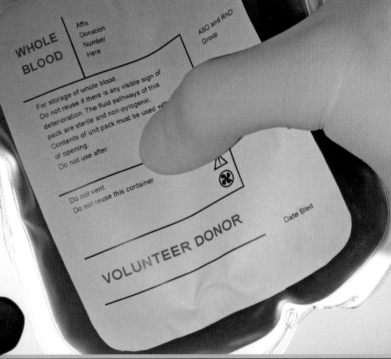

**People often donate blood to help others who are injured or sick.**

How does blood keep our bodies healthy and strong? And what is this sticky red stuff anyway?

## MANY DIFFERENT PARTS

Blood is a **suspension** that flows through our bodies in arteries and veins. Under a microscope, blood looks like many different cells bumping around in a pale liquid. The constant pumping of the heart keeps the different parts mixed up. But it is possible to separate those parts and study them one by one. Your different blood cells do different jobs, and each job is important.

 **suspension** a substance made up of many parts floating in a fluid

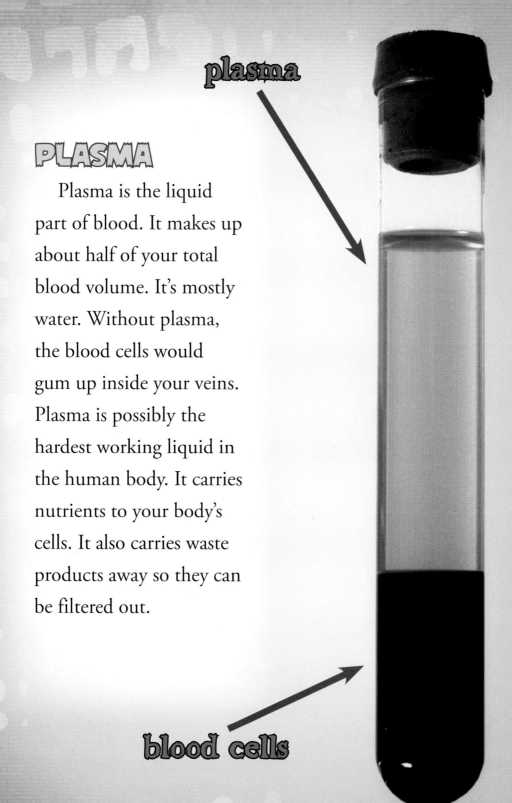

plasma

## PLASMA

Plasma is the liquid part of blood. It makes up about half of your total blood volume. It's mostly water. Without plasma, the blood cells would gum up inside your veins. Plasma is possibly the hardest working liquid in the human body. It carries nutrients to your body's cells. It also carries waste products away so they can be filtered out.

blood cells

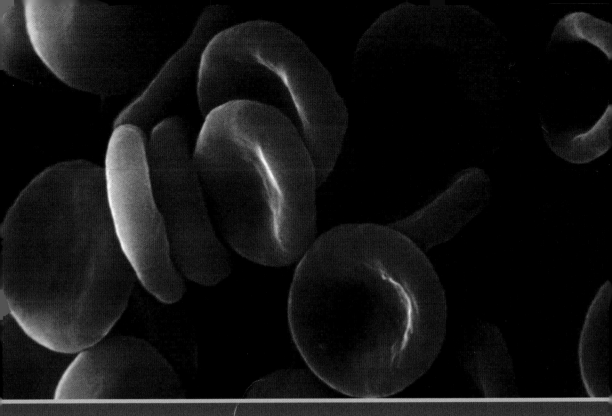

Red blood cells look like tiny discs with a dimple in the middle.

# RED BLOOD CELLS

Blood cells make up about 45 percent of the blood. Most of these cells are red blood cells. Red blood cells contain an iron-rich protein called hemoglobin. It's what causes your blood to look red. Hemoglobin binds oxygen to red blood cells. The cells then carry the oxygen to the rest of your body. Without red blood cells to carry oxygen, your body would die.

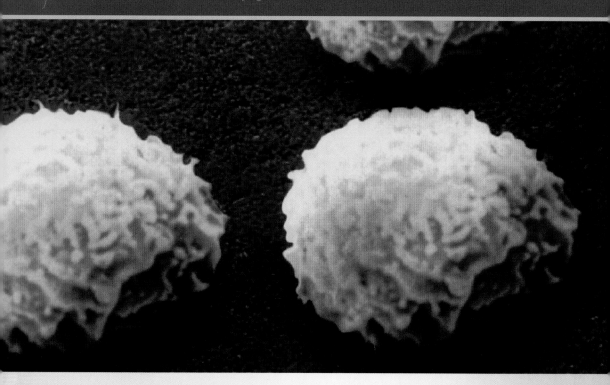

White blood cells are always ready to deal with sneaky germs.

## THE BODY'S POLICE

White blood cells make up less than one percent of the blood. Some white blood cells attack and destroy germs such as viruses. Others make **antibodies**. Some white blood cells also collect and get rid of dead body cells.

 **antibody** — a substance that kills germs

Platelets are another important blood cell. They're shaped like tiny eggs. When you're injured, platelets help create a net of protein fibers called fibrin. Red blood cells become tangled in the fibrin net to make a blood clot. Blood clots plug wounds to stop the bleeding. When the blood dries, it creates a scab on your skin. Scabs help keep nasty germs from entering your body through a wound.

**Platelets help make fibrin to create blood clots.**

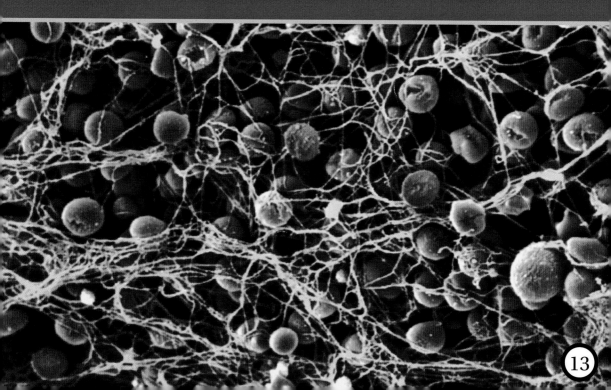

# BLOOD TYPES

Not all blood is the same. People have different types of blood. Normally, we don't have to think about our blood type. But if we need a **blood transfusion**, the issue of blood type becomes a matter of life and death. The four main blood types are A, B, AB, and O. If the wrong blood types are mixed together, the blood cells will attack one another. Patients who receive the wrong type of blood could die.

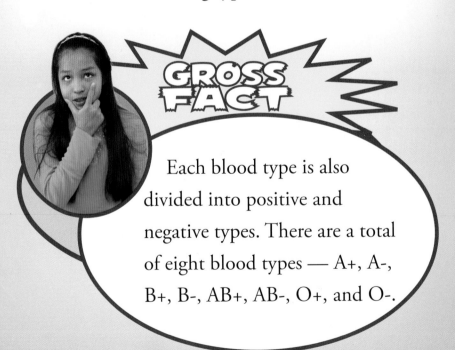

## GROSS FACT

Each blood type is also divided into positive and negative types. There are a total of eight blood types — A+, A-, B+, B-, AB+, AB-, O+, and O-.

**blood transfusion** transferring blood into a person after a bad injury or during an operation

During a blood transfusion, blood flows through a small tube into a person's body.

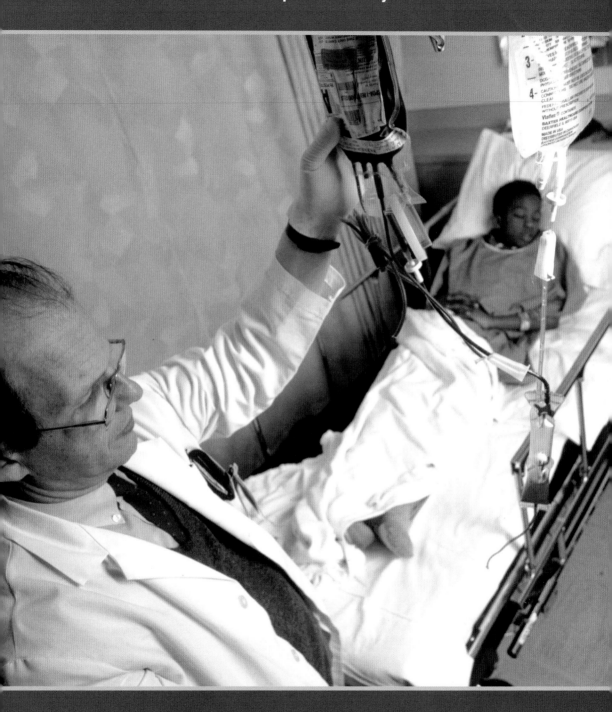

# HARD-WORKING BLOOD

We have a lot of blood flowing around inside us. But what does this mixture of plasma and cells do that's so important? You'd be surprised!

## OXYGENATION

Take a deep breath. Hold it for a moment. Now let it out slowly. While the air was in your lungs, your red blood cells trapped oxygen. This process is called oxygenation.

When the iron-rich hemoglobin in your red blood cells sucks up oxygen, it turns red. If you could see inside your body, you'd see your blood change from red-brown to bright red in your lungs. As the blood moves through your body, the red blood cells drop off oxygen to your body's cells. As it loses oxygen, your blood turns to red-brown again.

# THE BODY'S GARBAGE COLLECTOR

Blood also acts as your body's personal garbage collector. As your body's cells work, they produce waste products called **toxins**. These products include carbon dioxide and urea. In small amounts, these waste products aren't harmful. But in large doses, they can make your body's cells slow down and die.

Thankfully, the constant flow of blood carries toxins away from your cells. Blood carries carbon dioxide to your lungs where you can breathe it out. It carries urea to your kidneys. Your kidneys filter out the chemicals in your blood and turn them into urine.

**toxin** - a poisonous substance

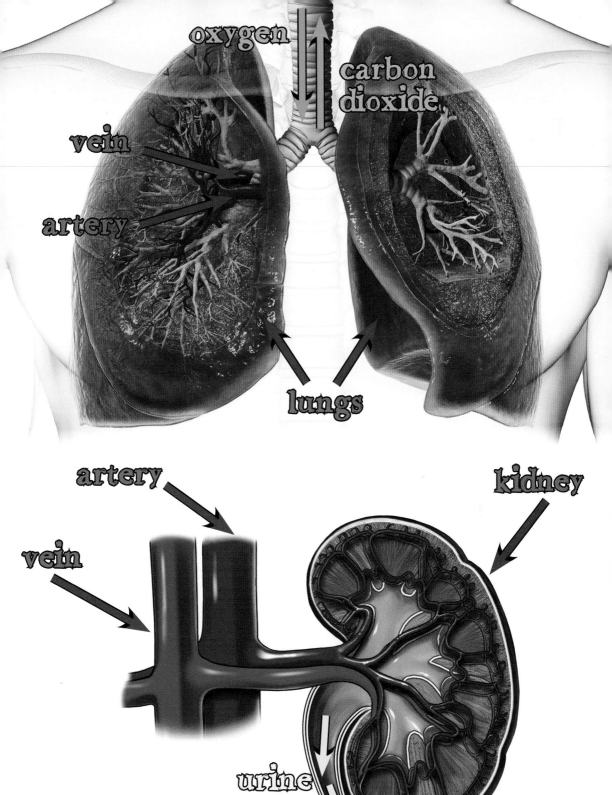

oxygen

carbon dioxide

vein

artery

lungs

artery

kidney

vein

urine

# SPEEDY DELIVERY!

Blood has one more important task. It delivers messages to other parts of your body. When we get hurt, our skin and blood vessels break and blood leaks out. Platelets quickly begin making a clot to stop the bleeding. But that isn't their only job.

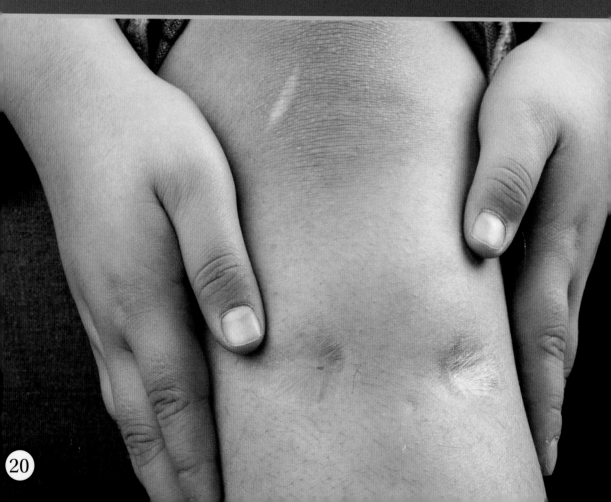

**Thanks to blood, wounds usually heal quickly.**

Platelets also release chemicals that tell the rest of the body that there is work to do. The white blood cells are told to begin attacking germs. And your body's cells get the message to begin fixing damaged tissue. These messages wouldn't be sent through your body without your blood. Remember that skinned knee you got last summer? It's gone, right? You can thank your blood for that!

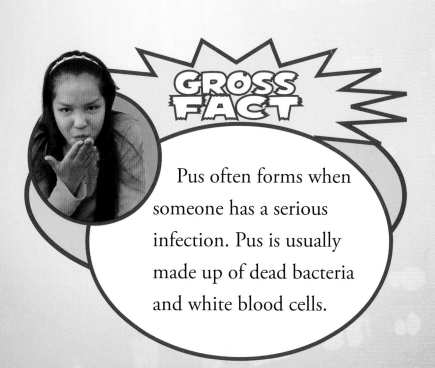

GROSS FACT

Pus often forms when someone has a serious infection. Pus is usually made up of dead bacteria and white blood cells.

# BLOOD TROUBLES

Small bruises can quickly grow huge
for hemophilia patients.

Blood is one of the hardest working substances in your body. But sometimes blood doesn't work the way it's supposed to.

## BLOOD DISORDERS

Hemophilia is a rare, but serious blood disorder. This disease keeps a person's blood from clotting properly. Patients with hemophilia need to be extra careful. A cut can bleed for days, and it may never completely heal. Even a small bruise can be a big problem. The extra blood pools under the skin, causing the bruise to grow to a huge size.

When people don't get the right nutrition, they can develop a sickness called **anemia**. For example, if people don't get enough iron, their blood can't carry enough oxygen to their bodies. People with anemia often feel very tired because their blood is low on oxygen.

 **anemia** a condition in which a person's blood doesn't carry enough oxygen to the body

# BLOOD-BORNE DISEASES

Blood can carry nasty diseases through your body. Hepatitis is a disease of the liver. People catch this disease when they come in contact with infected blood. If the disease isn't treated, the liver will eventually be destroyed.

The HIV virus causes a disease called AIDS. HIV attacks and destroys a person's white blood cells. AIDS patients often die from common illnesses because the disease destroys their bodies' natural defenses.

Ebola is one of the scariest of all blood-borne diseases. This deadly virus causes high fevers and massive internal bleeding. Soon, the patient's organs begin to shut down and liquefy. Before long, blood pours out of the patient's eye sockets, ears, mouth, and sweat glands. The death rate for the Ebola virus can be as high as 90 percent. Fortunately, Ebola is extremely rare.

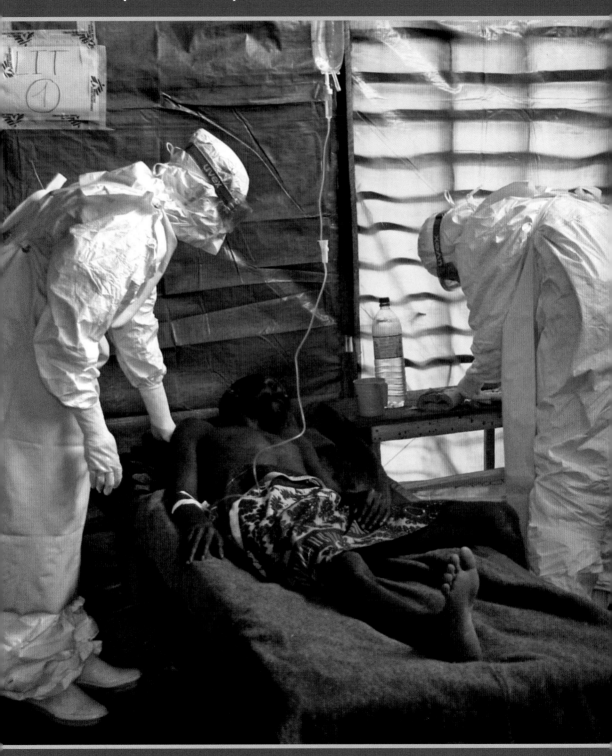

## HUNGRY FOR BLOOD

Several insects feed on human blood. These insects can spread many dangerous diseases. One common blood-sucker is the tick. Ticks will drink blood for days if they can. Some ticks carry diseases like Lyme disease. This dangerous disease can cause serious damage to a person's joints, heart, and nervous system.

Mosquitoes can also spread diseases. When a mosquito bites an infected person or animal, a little bit of infected blood stays in its snout. When it bites the next person, the blood gets injected into his or her veins.

Mosquitoes spread malaria in many tropical locations around the world. Malaria causes high fevers, joint pain, and vomiting. Bad cases of malaria can cause brain damage and even death. Millions of people are infected by this dangerous disease every year.

**Mosquitoes carry several dangerous diseases like malaria and the West Nile virus.**

# THANKS, BLOOD!

Some people feel sick at the sight of blood. Some people even faint when they see it. But blood isn't there just to be gross. Millions of tiny cells in your blood do very important jobs. They protect you from germs. They carry nutrients and oxygen to your body's cells. And they heal your wounds.

Without blood, a fun, healthy life wouldn't be possible. The next time you fall and scrape your knees, remember all the things your blood does to keep you healthy.

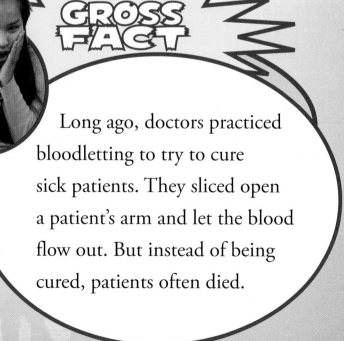

## GROSS FACT

Long ago, doctors practiced bloodletting to try to cure sick patients. They sliced open a patient's arm and let the blood flow out. But instead of being cured, patients often died.

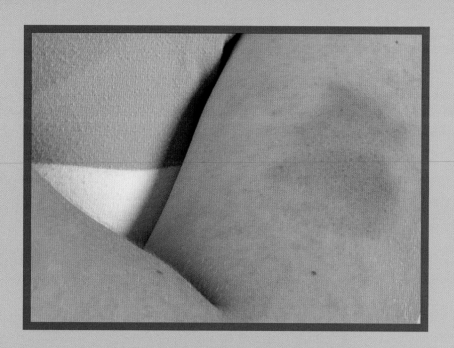

# WHAT'S A BRUISE?

Bruises form when the soft tissues under your skin are damaged. If you get hit hard enough, tiny blood vessels under your skin break. Blood then leaks out and pools under your skin.

At first, the spot might look red or purple, and it's probably pretty sore. Over time, your body reabsorbs the blood and the bruise fades away. Bruises usually disappear in about two weeks.

# GLOSSARY

**anemia** (uh-NEE-mee-uh) — a condition in which the blood can't carry enough oxygen to the body's cells

**antibody** (AN-ti-bah-dee) — a substance produced by white blood cells that fights infections and diseases

**artery** (AR-tuh-ree) — a blood vessel that carries blood away from the heart

**blood transfusion** (BLUHD trans-FEW-shuhn) — the act of transferring blood into a person

**fibrin** (FYE-brin) — protein fibers that help form blood clots

**hemoglobin** (HEE-muh-gloh-bin) — a substance in red blood cells that carries oxygen and gives blood its red color

**hemophilia** (hee-muh-FIL-ee-uh) — a health condition in which blood does not clot normally

**oxygenation** (ok-si-juh-NAY-shuhn) — the process by which oxygen is absorbed by red blood cells

**suspension** (suh-SPEN-shuhn) — a substance in which many particles are suspended; particles in a suspension can be separated.

**toxin** (TOK-sin) — a poisonous substance produced inside the body as waste

**vein** (VAYN) — a blood vessel that carries blood back to the heart

# READ MORE

**Alton, Steve.** *Blood and Goo and Boogers Too! A Heart-Pounding Pop-up Guide to the Circulatory and Respiratory Systems.* New York: Dial Books for Young Readers, 2009.

**Lew, Kristi.** *Clot and Scab: Gross Stuff About Your Scrapes, Bumps, and Bruises.* Gross Body Science. Minneapolis: Millbrook Press, 2010.

**Romanek, Trudee.** *Squirt! The Most Interesting Book You'll Ever Read About Blood.* Toronto, Ont.: Kids Can Press, 2006.

# INTERNET SITES

FactHound offers a safe, fun way to find Internet sites related to this book. All of the sites on FactHound have been researched by our staff.

Here's all you do:

Visit *www.facthound.com*

FactHound will fetch the best sites for you!

# INDEX